Free Verse Editions
Edited by Jon Thompson

System and Population

Christopher Sindt

Parlor Press
Anderson, South Carolina
www.parlorpress.com

Parlor Press LLC, Anderson, South Carolina, 29621

Library of Congress Cataloging-in-Publication Data

Names: Sindt, Christopher, author.
Title: System and population / Christopher Sindt.
Description: Anderson, South Carolina : Parlor Press, [2017] |
Series: Free
   verse editions
Identifiers: LCCN 2017038914 (print) | LCCN 2017044752
(ebook) | ISBN
   9781602358874 (pdf) | ISBN 9781602358881 (epub) | ISBN
9781602358898 (
   ibook) | ISBN 9781602358904 (mobi) | ISBN
9781602358867 (pbk. : alk. paper)
Classification: LCC PS3619.I5687 (ebook) | LCC PS3619.
I5687 A6 2017 (print) |
   DDC 811/.6--dc23
LC record available at https://lccn.loc.gov/2017038914

2 3 4 5

Cover design by David Blakesley.
Cover image: Daniel Von Aarburg. Unsplash.com. Used by
   permission.
Printed on acid-free paper.

Parlor Press, LLC is an independent publisher of scholarly and
trade titles in print and multimedia formats. This book is available
in paperback and ebook formats from Parlor Press on the World
Wide Web at http://www.parlorpress.com or through online and
brick-and-mortar bookstores. For submission information or to
find out about Parlor Press publications, write to Parlor Press,
3015 Brackenberry Drive, Anderson, South Carolina, 29621, or
email editor@parlorpress.com.

Contents

Into the same rivers we step and do not step, we are and are not
—Heraclitus

Despues de años mil, vuelve el rio a su cubil
—Spanish Proverb

System and Population

Headwater

briefly
during floods

streambed
assembling thunder

impacts
of the unnecessary

"Let it be my faith
too. That there is

an order"

bright and peopled—
weddings,

parties, systems
to be

studied—

dry dam captures
the freshet,

rising,

mock-orange
appearing as

weaponry,
tiny tabernacles

System and Population

Seal the river at its mouth
take the water prisoner
fill the sky with screams and cries
bathe in fiery answers

—Townes Van Zandt, "Lungs"

1.

Graph of the water table

This morning's children

At the confluence

Among whitewater

"Weaving of a figure
Unweaving, an art of
Unsaying"

Weave in torrent,
An outpouring

      Bitter cup
      Figured wind

On Christmas day

In tumult

2.

The undertow of these glances, arms entangling, embracing the rose of morning.

The world is not common here: a welcoming shiver, appliances dumped in the river and the rusting of this or that love—

My sisters and I are fishing, and I am practicing the day-glo smear of fish-eggs.

She says my care was a form of carelessness (there on the open bridge).

And the winding and unwinding: "water moving through subsurface material" or "what flows beneath the surface on its own path."

This might be a letter to the drowned ones—Charlie, Monica, Joseph, James—a tribute or tributary, elegy or testament.

Never posted, possibly never conceived.

Or, an article in the Sunday *Journal* with the headline: "underflow as tribute to injury catching on in westerns states."

They were leaning over the tackle box, niggling over worms. Barbed hooks.

Flyline, leaders, tippets, fisheggs and nymphs. Two days after Christmas, sheet-metal sky and shivery girls.

I stepped on a rusty stove lying under water, lost the ability to think, blood gushing as I pulled my foot from the river.

Past, past, past tense, river was full of garbage and rust, river was unprotected.

We confirm the value of the Pinus sabniana: 40-90 feet, broad, heavy cones, 3 needles in a bundle, grey.

John Muir: "No other tree of my acquaintance is so substantial in body and yet in foliage so thin and pervious to light."

Miwoks boiled twigs, bark, and needles into a strong tea. Foothill, Grey, or Digger.

To review:
        a) the grey pine keeps its powers inside
        b) I discovered the hospital and the rigging of my big toe.

Time and memory. Work in the present a type of sifting made fictional through missteps and definitions.

An affluent flows into a larger river or lake, as do the lines of mind and grammar.

One could also imagine gas and dust expanding away from a particular point in time and space, seeming to lighten its value,

and the poem too a kind of expansion.

An acquaintance that announces itself speaking its substantial body to the mountaineer.

An acquaintance that listens. That "it" might be overheard making an acquaintance: haggard, broad-bodied pine.

That the tree might not listen to the man beside the flowing affluent in the canyon above the river.

But here in the poem the pine might disappear along with the Miwok and the interpretation.

A river without water but retaining its words and definitions. The boy has never cut his toe and the bridge has never been built.

We could begin our story again as headwaters continually begin: I see myself nine years old now lying on the rock as two teenage girls examine and bandage the injury,

a ripped headscarf as a tourniquet, codes of behavior learned from television.

Now it begins to mist slightly through the canyon, the pines shifting in medium wind.

It was morning, two days after Christmas.

"time, time. It's time."

This eye is painting today in its socket. Running water, grey pine, sheet-metal sky.

3.

Engaged in direction,
ashamed by

entering, like others:

beneath
the ripples

(far apart, they put us):

beneath the afternoon:
"abyss-mal, the gap"

beneath swallows

and dragonflies:
winter:

an issuing

from the earth
(dampening prayer):

and so, this is
an authority

of the river.

4.

It is keenly beside us, the river, spreading
fine mist through the evening, freshwater
on your upper lip, breads and cheeses, blankets,
but the sand gets everywhere and
there are many stories and querying
directions at the confluence:
a screech owl lands on a rock, blends, does not
divorce itself, forces itself to become
indistinguishable. "'Originality' is
NOT either interesting or available to me."
For how long has there been this problem
of what is available to me?
Rock is always *next to*, the patient one.
The January canyon is clear
enough, wide in places drifting in pure
direction, restraint shown only by surveyors,
looking beyond their transits and clipboards,
the darkening sky unmooring its elements
piece by piece and filtering with the mist, stars
dimly fielded and felt as points.
My river doesn't roar, it opens as backdrop
to the dance bands of the '40s and '50s,
the digging of bulbs and bells
along the gauzy display, easy enough to say
but harder and harder to see through.
The two of us and our shadows
felt the words and their meanings gaping
along the river. In the photographs,
smiling bodies in bathing suits and sepia.
Now the surveyors allow for a final
meeting or scratching in the dirt, made
for them with purple chalk and rolled paper,
moistening in the mist of the bend.
All of the river's words may be replaced
at any time with other words, the moon-
sheen, strengthened by kissing

along the banks. Now, the river can be seen
as its own tenant, using the bed as anyone
might and traveling in acre-feet.
It is keenly beside us, its long, long journey
in time and space through darkness
and daylight, wisdom and ignorance,
annotations from the most
primary of texts, its own map and line,
the versions of the story varied and tidal,
never looking back, impossible not to see faces
in dark reflections, its bed is also
a place in which we tousled lie down.

Debris Haibun

"The earliest human immigrants to California came from the north more than ten thousand years ago. By the time they arrived, the present configuration of California's landscape was well established and broadly similar to that of today, albeit a bit wetter and cooler. These early settlers colonized the floodplains of California, with the largest populations concentrated along the resource-rich rivers of the northern half of the state."

redress immigration
so as to float

redress the floodplain
concentrate persons

(Jeffrey F. Mount)

5.

This was before the time of panning for gold.

They dug wild onion and garlic and steamed salmon and acorns.

They had civilization at the confluence of the north and middle forks—dance house, sweat lodge, granary, wikiups under black oaks.

They burned the underbrush—manzanita, ceanothus, blackberry—to access all year the hard seeds and bulbs: hazel nuts, pine nuts, tubers, and roots.

They gaffed spawning salmon from the side of the river and walked between villages: Chulka, Bisian, Didit, Hakaka, Chapa.

What was private to them? What obstructions, what violence?

They traded for fish with shell money and obsidian with the Washoe and the Miwok.

They ground acorns for mush in rock beside this river.

They fasted and sweated before the deer hunt.

They spoke a form of Penutian, and shared this with the greater Maidu to the north and the Miwok to the south.

What did they lie to each other about? What mistakes pretended in translation?

Nisenan: southern branch of the Maidu, meaning "man."

Anabranch: a diverging branch of a river that reenters the main stream or loses itself in sandy soil.

6.

water on the lens
hawks in smeared purple
bleeding scripture

I've been running
this elegy before

what funny listening of the river

                                        before true
                                        before true

"so much false
or waste news"

a bird in forever
listened here
next to the arroyo
next to the angels

  (a brook, creek, stream, watercourse)

"not a constant replay," these memories

of my father—pyramids, false-
cedars: bell-shaped

cones, bark used for huts
wood used for pencils

Calocendars decurrens:
evergreen, perfect

7.

He reaches toward the flow assuming knowledge of debris.

How does he reach into the river, floating above it so?

The runoff makes an entrance from the canyon walls, filters compelled by gravity.

Is it "traveling" that shamans do better than others?

He travels in trances. The others beside the river and his body waiting.

And "each 'word' a severed distinct thing."

They walk beside the river that would be under water, images of submersion, distinct branches and histories, holding hands on the beach, each word running off from the past.

The miners lived there, and danced there. He speaks of these facts as gifts, severed and returned.

He makes his art by listening, to the Stravinsky birds across the canyon, to the distant foamy drone of traffic on Foresthill Bridge, to the river's roar that fades after intense listening, or wobbles, as the flow increases or decreases.

To be the portion that ultimately reaches, to feel the loss of words in the dull wall of anger, the sun straining through a sheath of clouds.

The swallows weave and unweave near the confluence.

Flight above water, against the current.

Their flight is his praise.

Their flight adjusts his listening.

The roar can be heard from the bridge and also under water.

His art can hear your hand on the wheel, your severed words.

8.

The great
fir's
joyful
branches, home

to song
sparrows,
sweetness.
Come

swim
with me
in the drowsy
stream

beside
crumbling
sandstone.
"There was

a lure
in the woods
and river-
banks

that never
materialized."
Roots
used

in basketry,
high
in vitamin C.
Seek me

out,
make me
matter
by the bank:

appearances.

Public Law 89-161

To authorize the Secretary of the Interior to construct, operate, and maintain the Auburn-Folsom South unit, American River division, Central Valley project, under federal reclamation laws.

Be it enacted by the Senate and House of Representatives of the United States of America in Congress assembled, That, for the principle purpose of increasing the supply of water available for irrigation and other beneficial uses in the Central Valley of California, the Secretary of the Interior (hereinafter referred to as the "Secretary"), acting pursuant to the Federal reclamation laws (Act of June 17, 1902; 32 Stat. 388, and Acts amendatory thereof or supplementary thereto), is authorized to construct, operate, and maintain, as addition to, and an integral part of, the Central Valley project, California, the Auburn-Folsom South unit, American River division. The principal works of the unit shall consist of—

(1) the Auburn Dam and Reservoir with maximum water surface elevation of one thousand one hundred and forty feet above mean sea level, and capacity of approximately two and one-half million acre-feet;

(2) a hydroelectric powerplant at Auburn Dam with initial installed capacity of approximately two hundred and forty thousand kilowatts and necessary electric transmission system for interconnection with the Central Valley project power system. [...]

Sec. 6 There is hereby authorized to be appropriated for construction of the Auburn-Folsom South unit, American River division, the sum of $485,000,000 (1965 prices), plus or minus such amounts, if any, may be justified by reason of ordinary fluctuations in construction costs as indicated by engineering cost indexes applicable to the types of construction involved herein. There are also authorized to be appropriated such additional sums as may be required for operation and maintenance of the project.

Approved September 2, 1965.

9.

We stalked on the bank or slipped
downstream, into counter-currents
beside the giant serpentine.
And the fault-block sat patiently
beneath us, bemused by our winnowing
and demanding uplift. Families
piled into rafts, paddling
furiously together. Two girls
on the sandy bank—lotion, sun-
glasses, possessing what they know
to be the whole attention
of the human world.

Earlier, there had been a morning
mist over pooling water.
By noon, the dry air screamed
in the background as the roar
dimmed, screamed at the boy
in the shade casually watching
his sister and her friend, loyally
believing in their beauty,
their quantity of matter, becoming
the climate itself for a moment,
friendly to him in words he formed
and didn't speak, *fraternity,*
sorority, people loving

in silence and distance
beside the roaring.
On other days, he slept in midday
sun, giving in to the casual
brutality of that heat
and awakening to the canyon
a disappeared person among granite
and flow with vultures overhead,
dull black plumage, scanning the rocks

for carrion, breathless in flight.
The sky was white
as if the blue had been sheened

and hardened like a ceramic bowl.
"When the voice in writing lifts
into the language of itself speaking…
the truth of the made thing presides."
That truth carried floating
in branches, soaked
debris from up-river, finding
reach for right exposure, lasting only
in language now, beyond
the form of tanning girls,
beyond voice, beyond rock,
to the reach, to the wider inventories.

10.

The gospel rain hums through the canyon and water rises in the
    core-channel.
She hates the rain and walking in it. Her wet face turns away from
    the sky.
But in the roar she hears into the river and its fears.
She hears the silent song of sheltering wrens, sheltering hawks.

We are walking on the muddy path to salvation.
"We no longer live within a possible history."
The roaring contains versions of the story, seemingly accurate and
    completely wrong.
The roaring remembers suicides and drownings but also the birth of
    my daughter.

"I was obliged to cross many slous of the River that were very miry."
We walk together on the border imagining a song sung to the melody
    of rain.
A song that sings of the dead and unremembered, the severed and
    unmarked.
Valley Oak: 40-100 feet: stout and deciduous tree, deeply lobed.

The generous storm quickens.
It sings of war, torture, burning cities, executions.
"As waves, after all, do overwhelm."
Flowing there on the periphery, inside or out.

An alignment to ideals is ugly no matter which.
The unraveling storm is not your heart or the river's.
Instead, it might be compared to television or radioactivity.

A kind of terror delivered in consistent doses but to places
    unspecified.
Broadcasting without direction, as in this portrait from the Gold Rush:
Yankee Jim had been a deserter from a merchant ship sailing the coast
    of California.
He spoke the finest English but imitated the speech of the miners.

He claimed land in the mountains between the north and middle
  forks of the American.
He reported to town with large chunks of gold and covered his
  tracks leading back.
He shot trespassers on his claim with a buckshot rifle and left their
  bodies on the periphery.
Most accounts say he was later hanged in Bridgeport for stealing
  horses.

The storm delivers itself evenly through the canyon.
The water covers abandoned homesteads, barbed wire and rusted
  metal, exotic species.
The names and other words are largely missing, along with their
  sparkling discoveries.
Along with double-crossings and miry crossings, diversions from.

11.

So what can be
found inside   strange treatments
from the origin?

"All the windows
open to the sun."

Merganser's glossy body
bathing   prickly life
under calm

beneath ponderosas:
John Muir: "gives forth   finest music
to the winds."

Deep water
beside Murderer's   Bar, shifting
channels, the canyon

wren, its short
repeated *bzert*,   the way
it zigs and zags, adapted

(rapids, obstructions)

to trick and devour—
falsely glittering—bloody   fate,
fishy cellophane.

12.

Memories that storm and stay in granite poses.

Her laughter closed as the doors closed.

And my small self began making decisions, shining upon certain souls under black oaks.

In wintry March, the granite shifted ever so slightly, like a metaphor grinding its tenor and vehicle into slightly different associations: laughter like tinfoil, her striped shirt like spring rain, these decisions like backwater,

> "turned in its course by an obstruction, an opposing current, or the tide,"

> lobed leaves, hard wood, burning
slowly—
> predicate plus object, her look askance as the door closed.

Or predicate piercing the object. The very nature of looking allows its mystery in multiple interpretations: desire (fleeting or sustained), friendly confidence, or a kind of practicing with the face. After many years, they found themselves sitting outside a Starbucks in a suburban mall. Her husband had just quit his job in the tech industry. It was a hot summer day in California and the coast range blurred its browns and oranges in the background, dry summer grasses, pine, salt of the bay lingering under the irrepressible sky.

After twenty years, it is not right to say he "kept things from her." There simply isn't time for all the telling one wants to do.

1974, George Rouse: "The results of my investigations indicate that a thin, double-curvature arch dam is not a suitable structure for the site when dynamic earthquake loadings are considered, and that the cracked dam could fail."

In Leigh's dream, the river is running with tea, and it's her job to capture it and serve it with suitable formality to a group of venture capitalists. Of course, she has no cups, no saucers, no sugar.

The census of syllables drowned in the roaring of the river. What he cried out for had lost its interlocutor. And if this survey of his thoughts might include her grammar, the opposing current would find its way in parentheses and stammering.

The numbers of water droplets in our imagination, binding to faces. The story must move (nervously) along a channel and say nothing. We were walking through a thicket of scotch broom, and I was talking about the relation of story to meaning. Years earlier, Rachel ran alongside me near Lake Clementine as I recounted the plots of novels. She was offering through her listening. She was looking up the canyon at a grove of black oaks, their brittle yellow leaves actually floating through the air, dampness in the small of her back.

When he closes his eyes the words are written in white lettering on a royal blue screen, fluttering. Richter scale, seismicity study, faults near the foundation, the "tremendous weight of water in the reservoir."

Faces applied to bodies there through the ruptures, as meanings withstand use and violent activity, preaching across distances he calls relationships.

> "Formal feeling"
> beloved form of river
> "not formal"
> beloved
> "consciousness"
> as a memory of blue
> "is the seed of art."

A town built of ruptures and the fear of them.

Those memories in granite, that drive to the corner bakery where she worked, flour and sugar and the clean, earnest smell of fresh bread, off the scale, returning to others by a different route, a town beside a canyon built during a rush for gold.

Summer morning, dusty oats, deep dryness of the oak, penetrating blue, sweat, black dog in direct sun, microscopes, poison oak, running the trails, mountain lions, blackberries, end of summer, sadness.

Debris Haibun

"The cohesive attraction between molecules of water also means that there is a direct connection between you and your watershed, through hundreds of miles of pipes, treatment plants, aqueducts, reservoirs, and rivers. Continuous 'ropes' of water may extend from a San Diego faucet all the way to the northern Sierra Nevada and the Colorado Rockies. 'Pull' from your end and water molecules transmit that tiny force, reacting all the way up the line."

Morning attractions
I met the broken runner

Carve a pattern
The earliest inventor

(David Carle)

13.

Magnitudes! Liquid pronouncements! A town built of measurements. But there is the oracle oak, there is history in running water. The story is the sound of ceaseless running, promissory, devotional to acre feet and prior appropriation.

My listening will fade to watery pastels and falter, or my listening will pool and deepen, but falter. "All the living must tremble." The red-tailed hawk falters in a westerly gust and lands on the branch of a pine: a shrill, long whistle, measurable sound cascading upon trembling prey.

14.

If you call a thing a canyon
you are saying a thing continues to deepen
despite contemporary theory and John Ashbery.
And said canyon is, in fact, eroded
evidence of the interior, the fragile surface
to be lost in another season,

                 the effluent
containing the history of the epoch
and its unraveling, the niche surface
temporarily interesting but only in its connection
to granite and the Pacific, its being delivered.
Or you might find teenagers on the surface
drinking beer and diving from high rocks.

                 Or a family
in unstable aluminum
chairs and shivering suits. So what
thing calls out to the open canyon?
How does it sing?
The thing is a granule of sediment
and it sings by moving, and you can

                 count the granules
to hear the song
of this surface. In other words,
you can't hear the song of this surface.
What other creature in starry vestment
can hear the arrangement of this calling?
The performance itself stands

                 at the juncture
between text, preparation, the history
of the performers, lighting, instruments,
and audience, each with its own fault-lines
unknown to any one listener.

But you take this constancy
as your unlawfully wedded heart, encouraging

                    slippage, cracks
in red clay. How deep does the fissure run?
You might say it deepens in time,
but in this sentence, "it" is more than a crack. You
might say it radiates from a bone-hard center,
like a decaying diamond. You might say
there is no bone-hard center at the base

                    of the fissure,
so that it becomes a kin to the television
news, repeated views of war across the surface
and above bottomlessness, saturated, drowned
in (or by) dusky depth. You might imagine
our distance from love makes the current
easier or more difficult to navigate.

                    The moments
of entry into rushing water, yes,
but how can this distance
describe our immersion?
The aluminum chairs are scraping
against river rock. And to immerse yourself
in love is to love immersion.

                    Distance from
love can drown you in the depths
on this winter day here along the north fork
of the American in the shadows of the blue oak.
Or take the concept of headwater:
the source of a river which is another kind
of depth, historical and metonymic,

                    to touch
what companions the future, as if
reaching back with the urge to propel.

Imagine a river that does not carve a channel.
This expands our view of companionable depth,
targets the mind does not know but does, water
that "springs from" a certain locale

                        under the surface.
And this futile depth is invented here
in the canyon out of the human
construction of time, memory,
and the inference of the same. "There has been
no time in human history
that was not a time of war," or a time of

                     war remembered,
the WAR against the BIRDS, against
INSECTS, WAR against REPTILES,
the WAR of POETRY against the crushing
virtues of REPRESSED
IMAGINATIONS, and many others.
This you discover beside the river

                     listening: that
the surface is denial
and its exploration a repression of time or
interiors. And you're not always beside
the river coarsely listening. These "colored
and distorted lenses" revealing that
what you see is a revelation

                     of largesse
that your mind participates in
expanding, like a symphony or a garbage heap.
Is this or that quality of the river
a shadow that we cast?
Do these qualities find companionship
in the bluish foliage, in the depth

                     of the forest?

34

You don't know. You might say
the fault-line in the canyon changes
your behavior more than the earth's crust.
You might say you know where the river is
running and where it's been, fast-forward
and reverse, illusory depth, blank walls.

15.

Charles Leander Weed first appeared in Sacramento in 1854 and became a camera operator in the daguerreotype portrait studio of George J. Watson. In 1858 he was the junior partner of Robert Vance with a studio on J Street. In September of that year he photographed fluming operations along the middle fork of the American. At this time, thirteen miles of the river were flumed with rough-hewn pine and canvas, 10,000 men mining along the stretch. The photographs were used by Thomas Armstrong to make wood-cuts for *Hutchings California Magazine* in 1859 and 1860.

In September 1858, a storm flooded the canyon, washing out the fluming operation before the men had a chance to mine the dry bedrock. Timber and canvas were strewn along the shore for miles.

By the time these photos were taken, Weed had switched from daguerreotypes to the wet collodion technique that would be introduced at the California State Fair a few years later. One photograph captures the tunneling operation common at the time: a short track running from a bored tunnel in the hillside to a stilted terminus hanging above the canyon near the river. A small car was filled with diggings from the tunnel, and the image predicts that the car will run along the track and dump the waste diggings into the river channel. Weed captures the geometric precision of the tunnel, tracks and buildings, contrasting it with the wildness and destruction of the natural world around it: freshly cut dirt, down trees, and haphazardly constructed houses along the ridge.

These tunnels were common in the canyon when I was growing up and have only recently been boarded or closed. I explored them with my friends, up to our thighs and sometimes swimming in the underground pools: rusty water, flashlights, dripping red clay sweating from tunnel walls.

"his yearning
for the genuine is

a freezing,
a crystallization."
Eroding song, shimmery
and wet, bless me
into negative
exposure.

16.

Seismic study
How well did we
How well did we crumble
Concrete gravity

Pool below
Canyon oak
Safe design
What angers you so?

"Overgrown mind"
Breaks you
Your golden scale
Your implements

Redacted sections
Steelhead swimming
Your shimmerings
Reports and specimens

On August 1, 1975, a 5.7 Richter magnitude earthquake occurred near Oroville, California. This event suggested the possibility that part of the old Foothills Fault System south of Oroville might be active. At the time of the earthquake, the foundation for Reclamation's concrete arch dam at Auburn was being excavated and treated.

Because the Auburn damsite is centrally located in the Sierra foothills a seismic study was initiated by Reclamation in September 1975 to determine if a new earthquake evaluation was required. The study showed that reevaluation of the seismic data for the design of Auburn Dam was necessary [...]

Because of the remote possibility that an earthquake of engineering significance might possibly occur in the vicinity of the site during the life of the dam, the planned Auburn Dam was redesigned to meet higher seismic standards.

Auburn Dam Report (1985)
Prepared bt the U.S. Department of the Interior
Bureau of Reclamation/Mid-Pacific Region

17.

The great blue heron reminds us of deserved riches: encyclopedia, liquid breath, packing tape. Its harsh croak unburies elementary memory, fish and mice along canals and inlets.

The retired nurse hangs clothes on the line, sunny day in the canyon, sustaining love for unnamed birds. The naturalist attends to the day, the sky like a white wound, dusky cedar and pine, the ribboning river like a weight at the base of the canyon.

We were warned about these natural processes. You want to speak to your other, your wanderer, your broken one, to focus your attention on a single being.

This morning you are thinking of money and arguments, the gorgeous symbols within the system, pyramids and weights, chandeliers, eagles, the congressional seal, the price tag for the dam reaching 2.2 billion: signatures and debts, public and private.

Was capital enough to supply the concrete?

"Love is nature to nature and your being is what sustains me here, not your deserving."

The bird's blue reminds us of riches to be packed outside of commerce, stillness along the bank's deepening color, our eyes waiting for those quick and awkward departures.

The naturalist looks askance and preserves the color in his sketchpad, small fear lingering in his fingers. The heron lifts her head to the dreaming and finds green slopes and human frailty, the roar, the blackberry, flashes of fish, appropriations and classifications in summer light.

And they speak in birdcalls, using instruments when necessary for communication.

Wanting to travel without red direction. The canyon tinged with dust, little jetties and inlets, the nurse's beige sweater fallen from the line. The various castings and twistings (embracings) of our dreams, the mulberry tree, the nascent trail to the view. Stories of the singers of the canyon who lost their tongues in drawings. The sculpture she made was soon to fall and break: three coils, a laundry clip, and a chalk drawing of a heron.

And the groundwater within the earth that supplies wells and springs, good intentions.

The naturalist reaches into the canyon as far as his arms can reach. The heron covers a larger nature.

18.

War, and rebuilding from it,
"as always."

The lonely ones wait by the shore.
The lonely ones embarrassed lie

down by the shore. Awesome commerce
here within the river's allowance, its way

of roiling in many directions,
dying and living at once.

Cost-sharing for water projects,
local sponsors.

We might find solace in the live oak
"Tho we may live

with our homes and personal lives
not immediately under attack."

We notice one branch flows into
another, bigger river.

The lonely ones and our notebooks,
one peaceful word

under attack from another
peaceful word. Toothed

leaves, roosting for
quail, center of solace.

19.

I want to ground the grey and green
to silt, expose the speckled oxides. I want
to sever my skin with jagged rock. I want
the wordy silt to bleed like knowledge into fissures.
But remember the river and its revelations,
its pursuit through narrow channels, sedimentary
rock sentrying next to quaking
aspens. Quaking the thing her body does,
shuddering like rock when language tumbles out.

"I'd mail you my actual heart."
I've been waiting beside the fraying shirt.
One hundred miles to the frith, this opening
to the sea. I was there floating
without eyes, suspended over the churning,
trains along the edge, cold-cold air, heron-blue
water below, weightless but resisting, my actual
heart throbbing through fraying bedclothes.
I decided to follow another in flight
to the river's edge, and my breathing was another's

breathing seen from beside the world.
Bechtel recommends a straight design,
architectures of dreamy resistance,
as if a man and a clean clipboard
could fill the air with pencil lines, hold back
the river with his imagination, his car idling
on the fire road. But for now
the stranded dam-site is home
to fog and fishing lines, abandoned
debris and resistance, hearty waiting.

The globe-lily bends by the weight
of rainwater filling its lantern, casting
its light on the unknown by the banks.
I took its delicate, nodding neck in my hands

and leaned beside it. The flowers stand
for the canyon's power to animate, put
a glow into the darkness, provide for
roomy conversation when no one is building
anything. And the lilies found the
rain exhilarating, yes, and nourishing, yes.

The body was trembling but the actual heart
felt like demonstration plastic, smearing
leakage in the seams, circuits of memory,
circuits of pain, her body trembling, lost
in the river, renderings of flags, targets, numbers,
"things the mind already knows," and the river
following the bed it already knows,
the lover's body neither noticed
by the canyon nor changed by any
accuracy we might call a bulls-eye.

The canyon pulled light from the funnel
of sky like a father. A theory of loss
designed to work itself into the population,
unused and neutral, the funneled light
seeming to laugh as it travels from sky
to river, darkening without permission
from us or them or the birds or fish.
But now I am moving here on the shore, my
actual heart and winter dullness, things
needing to be used where they stand, her body

trembling there in the withholding twilight,
not appearing exactly, not as a body
coming around the corner, like a mannequin.
"She loved plastic persons," the brittle hair,
blonde that turns to sandy when wet,
the comedy of things as they are strewn about
and left by accident: dolls, hairclips,
pebbles moved from place to place in the pockets
of children, each hard little body resting there,
each calendar marked for this day, and this next one.

Now the site itself assembles, channeling
unrelated soils into one flowing,
historical and geological,
"things they look for in triage."
There is now a mucky bed where
the shoreline once was, the river has jumped,
the size of a door and its pooling rooms,
painted grey and proclaiming its own
decoration, the stand of grasses
blocking my access to the bend,

where birds still act like birds, skimming
the surface for prey instead of standing for
something like nobility or frailty. And the day
works its transition into dusty twilight, grey
pines shouldering the loose red dust,
and then later in darkening night,
lessoning and disappearing into the mass
of hillside. It's not her body trembling
now but its the actual laboring, the measured
breathing here, beside the actual river.

20.

From the tanning rocks beside the repaired cofferdam:

In winter an inlet brook drops down the canyon wall and enters the American, darkening in daylight and then disappearing into the trees.

Constellation under water, blurry bodies, settled and softened by the rapid current. Serpentine chips from canyon walls east of here, travelers. When you stand on them, you rest in their cooler hardness.

Buckeyes along the shoreline: *Aesculus californica*, crooked branches, showy flowers, shrubbery. Pomos leached their poisonous seed and stunned trout in pools. In spring the blossoms look like spiky urchins, deadly to honey bees, roots binding soil along the shoreline.

And the river is written in a language without translation on which bedrock sits quietly or moves out of the way, marbling but vital.

The shoreline of bystanders so frayed by observing they miss the cooling fish nipping the glassy surface.

Your friend waves and passes quickly, boulder to boulder and wading, fishing trout, the fly and line curving like a nerve in orange light as he casts and reels and disappears in sunset haze around the bend.

Vitus californica: wild grapes vined in place just behind the small beach. Cool, heart-shaped leaves like tissue. We walked back there in the 80's to be alone among the tangles and bitter fruit. Afterward, we gathered the grapes and rinsed them in our naked hands.

A long way to Folsom, a long way to the delta. Dusky nights when the American is a dark vault moving beneath reflection, spiky destinations.

Debris Haibun

"While the great majority of the world's large dams and all of the major dams have been completed in the last six decades, some of the environmental effects of a dam may not be realized for hundreds of years after construction. A dam can thus be regarded as a huge, long-term and largely irreversible environmental experiment without a control [...] The most significant consequence of this myriad of interconnected environmental disruptions is that they tend to fragment riverine ecosystems, isolating populations of species living up and downstream of the dam and cutting off migrations and other species' movements. Because almost all dams reduce normal flooding, they also fragment ecosystems by isolating the river from its floodplain, turning what fish biologists call a 'floodplain river' into a 'resevoir river.' The elimination of the benefits provided by natural flooding may be the single most ecologically damaging impact of a dam. This fragmentation of river ecosystems has undoubtedly resulted in a massive reduction in the number of species in the world's watersheds."

Offering an ending
Or no ending

Cheap cheap go the
Alarms and tanagers

(Patrick McCully)

21.

desire for beginning
unending

speckled granite
damp tanager

efficient
domain

gang of sparrows
forming

resources unending
beginning

22.

"Just here, here and here"

Yellow flowers spreading their populations across the field. The church is imagined, sixty feet into the branches. The sum of all things realizes "grief was enacting itself." The church records the smell of abandonment. The sum of all things lifts its face to the wind. The church smells like adult loneliness. The tree measures innumerable cubits upon cubits. The dog lifts its head to the wind above the canal. Straight as a gait. Here the flowers are nearly flowers. Just here, in morning sun, the flowers enacting themselves. When we dissolve into the maple we are dizzy with the fragrance of all things.

23.

War upon war,
quelling resistance.

Internet specializes
in this

inundation, population
without end.

The history that washes
and replaces.

Tibet, China, Tibet, China,
"that generation

of a history I barely bring
into existence,"

autonomy,
independence, resistance.

Spirits pass busily
beside grey pines,

toyon and star thistle
just coming into bloom.

Brodiaea: tight cluster of flowers
on a long single stem, hillsides,

bulbs, food for Nisenan:
raw, fried, boiled, or roasted.

Free water: ground water
that moves against gravity.

24.

That wispy cloud was a soft report,

the redbud's
      heart-leaves
            burdened

with dew. They walked quietly

back to the overlook to kiss,
bound
      by that, they were
            awakened
and the parking lot ran off in sun-stained

directions, stories
of her
      grandmother's
            native French.
Revitalized in the wake of our beloved

ideas, a price for national elections
(*pale red,*
      blue banners,
            white conference),
water still cascading over these

steeply slanting rocks, invigorating
itself
      after falling apart
                against
solids, the idea of building

this multipurpose (*unspeakable*)
has been
      revived
            in committee.

This voice was the voice of a woman

in her nightdress whispering in many languages
(*French,*
        Arabic,
                Swahili)
the advancing of this channel,

the candle on her nightstand
beside restful
                curtains, and
                                the gospels
where the house rested, and rested again,

children's rooms, quarreling rooms, diagrams

(*design,*
                diversion)

of flowers and hearts, the sketchpads

she called her only reliable lovers.
The music is,
                playing is,

playing recorded music is,

this interlude is, the melody is
matching
                the flow
                      and drift of this
river. These two channels

 are movement not bodies

(*as the*
        violin
                and viola

are bodies, not music),

blending particles and history,
bridge
            abutments
                        and rusted metal

(faded newsreel, microfiche),

graveyards and fireplaces,
local
            and entrepreneurial
                                    failures.
But the future is silvery

and pre-televised, the politician
quoting
            Whitman quoting
                            Emerson,

(Kanuck, Tuckahoe, Congressman, Cuff).

The wild grape is here, and the st. johnswort,
the nonnative
                    cypress
                                beside the old
homestead foundation, all the beloved

river-side weeds, standing like gifts
to be
            forgotten: a
                            revanchist biota
soon blossoms: this speech is loud

until there is no where else to bloom.

("I mean
            to spend

                                        more time
with the plant world.") And from this side

of the divide, a memory of plants
awakening. It's time

for green tenderness, mash of

thumbprint, whispers there
at the base
                        of the spring,
                                        rock
worn from the bed, this election

of shoreline, this temporary
boundary,
                        recorded in charcoal

                                        languages,
whispers of the leaf-body.

Direct Impacts in the Upper American River Area

With the selected plan and the 400-year alternative, the construction impacts would occur at and around the existing multipurpose Auburn Dam site [...] Operation of a flood control dam near Auburn would temporarily alter the visual and recreational quality of the inundation zone. During a large flood event, this area would become a reservoir for several days depending on the size of the storm. These infrequent temporary inundation events could result in gradual changes in the composition of the plant communities within the inundation zone due to the physiological effects of flooding. Periodic filling and emptying of the canyon could also cause soil slips along the canyon walls in the inundation zone. These slips would destroy vegetation, mar the physical appearance of the canyon, and disturb existing archeological sites.

Feasibility Report
U.S. Army Corps of Engineers
and the Reclamation Board, State of California
December 1991

25.

I'm running in the pre-dawn chill on the trail just above the
confluence, trail and river still in shade, the water's surface reflecting
canyon-sides and up to sun-line, Van Gogh yellows and greens.
And further up the canyon wall, ponderosas stand like citadels and
one wild healthy ceanothus grows directly from a crack in a massive
slab of serpentine. Pain in the hands and ears, liquid breath,
dripping creek, damp earth.

"It's all here [in Boehme], the underlying acknowledgement of a
wholeness in which all that we see and hear in nature, the figures
and sounds of heaven and hell are in-bound: that what we feel right
now if we bare ourselves nervously and sympathetically to evidences
of human beings—as if it were a river of the species and had in one
current the cruelty and the kindness, the stupidity with malice and
the wisdom, etc.—to be felt with love must be fearful."

The acknowledgement of a wholeness here in a tree or rock, in the
bend of the river. A type of language speaking itself in unique form.
The way the flow pushes away to my right against the embankment
and then the delicate slow pull down to the left, counterbalancing.
This might be considered a style, inscribed in rock long ago
(nostalgia for this bend in the river!), but with only parts of the
memory accessible, the curvature, color, speed, the slight roaring,
familiar. Remnants of.

A man loves these remnants, becomes a geologist, then a
hydrologist, finds a job at the local irrigation district. Despite his
love for the facts of the canyon, he is blamed in the newspapers for
this or that shortage. His opposition to the dam becomes public
and he is accused of siding with environmentalists and mountain
bikers. And of sentimentality. Worst of all, he must sit in meetings
in Sacramento or Washington talking about who owns what water.
The experience leads to dissociation and dissonance, and then a
deepening of respect for the resilience of the canyon, and then
eventually a new state of acceptance.

In his retirement, he becomes a lover of Schubert, especially the sweet melodies contained in his *Unfinished Symphony*. He begins to see the shape of music in the river, not a soundtrack to motion but the rock and water in motion, expressing an emanation in style. The river sings without notation—in this way (via), it speaks of its own operatic creation and experience: cruelty and kindness, stronger attractions, fearful love.

26.

Threatening evacuation
"I garden like I write or talk, into

densities. Overgrown mind." Madrone:
broadleaf, redhead, mealy pulp and scaly bark.

To the cool baldness of the Madrona!
If my private life

were to become too   (cataract!)
If my audience with others intensified

If I remained under water—
"The whole is the false," writes Adorno.

Tens of thousands of people,
vulnerable to fire and discharge.

The Maidu made lotion from the same leaves
settlers ground for gunpowder.

27.

Orange-rose, filtered and leafy:

the silk-screened tree, she:

into the belly of a long, long:

earthy arrival, stirring cocktail:

emotion instead of reason:

the water and changing, yes:

as is, as is delivered:

escape, fomenting:

soul, nimbly along:

future pathways, channels:

this or this or this, that:

she was there by the jetty:

she wants but does not say:

the answer: "goodbye":

empty clothesline:

of water pooling, toxic:

"at the most important crisis:

we had tried to overlook:

some obstruction in our selves:

that what we love:

flourish in its own character:

 to 'correct' us—":

Then her red answer:

Then her second red answer:

why can't those dreams fade away:

he meant forgetting:

popcorn flower, white:

would she sit quietly while he talked:

white flowers in spiral:

and say what, what then, and then:

spiral or coil, purple stems:

discursive intellect is the sixth sense:

an embroidered daisy:

on my daughter's dress, electric violin:

Chester listened to chamber music:

after the event, after the liberation:

2002: the SS guard confesses:

your feelings about that a type of prayer:

standing in the garlic farm under cypresses:

he speaks French, he speaks German:

alone in his cellar, he is silent for a season:

bodies, and body fragments:

most are shapes to us and others:

then he types and signs the program:

then he types a letter to his father:

we don't feel it but we know:

how it is supposed to feel:

we don't resist:

we don't resist your story:

granite, asteroid:

others are not here:

they are the government:

there is a word for this outside:

she crocheted table-cloths:

others were there in the village:

she resisted:

she was there by the jetty:

delivered there, bodies and fragments:

we don't feel it but we know:

river rock, smooth with time:

28.

A little heart
written in pebbles
beside California laurels.

Spreading branches
into filtered brightness, spicy
foliage, menthol for rubbing

compounds, medicinal:
to stimulate growth or multiply.
"Rebels without factories

shut down factories of the self."
The way the heart can simply shut down.
Drunken boys from town.

(bottles clinking)
The deeper part of a working body
letting main currents flow.

Debris Haibun

"Flooding in the Sacramento Valley long antedated the heyday of the gold rush era and remained a serious problem generations after mining had fallen on hard times. Early attempts to grapple with the problem illustrate how water overabundance has frequently been as serious as shortage […] As former miners turned to cultivating the rich soils, they discovered the awesome power of the Sacramento River, which regularly transformed the valley into a vast inland sea a hundred miles long that usually persisted well into summer, with much of the valley remaining swampland year round."

The trees hold their toxins
Inside, like people

Efficient sobbing
Local swamp

(Norris Hundley, Jr.)

29.

Chances 'have never been
better' for this

covering of land

not usually covered, the idea that

trapping a resource
saves others

from it, and saves it for us

for later use by children
and landscaping.

Nothing can be

erased completely, no,
not even

the foundation

of the tabernacle, pieced
with sand and weed-

beautiful seeds—

the losses
that cling next to

the river-mind,

'environmental solution'
during moments

of reflection,
when I drive
to vantage points

on the ruin—
"staking out claims
in nowhere." I reflected

on the goldfields:
reddish stems, narrow leaves,

orange-head at the end

of yellow petals, multitudes.
And then the dream began,

the origin dream, the flooding
for the first time

of this canyon. I was designing

water flow, a way
to measure impact

and assess the damages

to the populations: water-skiers and
fishers, irrigators

and speculators,
in congruence or opposition

to reason.

Constructed for us
and in us and wherever it need be

found, after

the instruments, after the implements,
after the earth-movers.

30.

Ranunculus eschscholtzii, poisonous to all:
little frog, lemon-yellow, first in spring, seedy cereal.
To be felt with love, this breeze, this wholeness—
We confirm the three segments, deeply
parted, large petals—we bare ourselves

to these along the river, kneeling to the straight stalk.
We sketch in charcoal, this and the other
flowers. The rootstock expands underground
in mysterious networks. "Miles of river canyon
into a reservoir." This sounds good

enough, description ignoring the creatures
at dawn and creatures at midnight, creatures
in cold winter and creatures in summer
solstice, all the effort to live, a million
sewing machines! And the American always

nearby and the abandoned homestead there
in its decaying foundation.
The buttercup stands there laughing
among its friends, cheerful and straight
in this field of competitors, the in-bound

sounds of heaven and hell.
The frenzied mind lost
in opposites, the unforgiving
mind and its vocal hearts, their systems
nowhere in the long meandering.

To be felt with love.
To stand with your questions
among the different styles.
To stand by the ford
with another of your species.

31.

Canyon beneath foundling sky, graying to blue

after saw-toothed sunset. Not fussy about perfections

or even happiness among the stinging nettle. The souring

sky reaches for its firth: "as if I ought to feel

pain, despair, deadly boredom." Fishing

line, barbed wire, broken glass. The thread of the whole

river calming the breath. A person has no choice

when he wants everything. Stinging

and allowing another to sting.

32.

The river's heart is still through white water.

The veined patterns of discourse.

Devastation written in the air and blueprints.

EPA or Interior, or the City of, the County of.

Hot summer day, ripened blackberries.

Each item ruffling its dusty course.

I want to sing in my own true course.

Define course as a channel through which things flow.

Define channel as tired choices hardened over time.

Her living and my living, mapped and helpless.

Redbud near the shoreline, patterns in baskets, tea.

Define flow as living without reflection.

The barely perceptible mist that dampens potential.

Sediment moving without reflection.

Or these distressed travelers pausing on the bank.

Singing whispers and distressed replicas of thought.

Or chattering their misrememberings in loud voices.

Working figures reflected in the shallows, kicking sediment.

The redbud is flared and silent beside the shallow news.

The river withholds its information.

"There is a clear necessary red flow of the stream."

> The necessary and clear
> Might restrict the seer

Then continue the litany of flared and silent words.

Redbud browning on the leaf-edge.

He sits with legs crossed on the shoreline with vultures overhead.

He remembers his underwater lacerations.

The red flow hums to the history of this river.

Songs like these, stream-like in their meandering and dull noise.

The "clear necessary" can be read in our conversation and in our silence.

And in these things: tree, river, bodies, words between us:

> A hum like a genotype
> The dance of words and spray

He would comprehend or not, but regardless he would explain.

All of the risks to this pristine garden, or shall we call it wilderness?

Darkening in afternoon, shall we call it world?

Debris Haibun

"Water wars are global wars, with diverse cultures and ecosystems, sharing the universal ethic of water as an ecological necessity, pitted against a corporate culture of privatization, greed, and enclosures of the water commons."

Cloud without slope
Water is energy

Binoculars
Starry yearnings

(Vandana Shiva)

33.

Or push
                    forward
down, down,
down

beyond drowning
beyond
        ignorance

of the editorialists
and ignorance of the non-
                    voting "woods
                    and river banks,"

poisonous
larkspur.

34.

The river descends
with its cold ignorance, moving
steadily down
but pausing left and right, asserting
stillness or rest from the cold grey sky
and the silence of the canyon, part of
the fluid body continuously moving
in certain direction, current
which sometimes deadens
the issues—your family
on the bank with its seismic activities,
containing this or that like bowls
or stove-pots, this laughter
followed by speeches and yearning—
and then the violet-blue larkspur
appears. This poison cannot kill
this "life" at the river, persistent,
risky. The air is nothing
but the something
that anything is, temperature and wind
and feelings made of color.

Politician or journalist, citizen activist: you know how
this works: the USGS issues a review that declares
the river more volatile "than previously reported."
The rock wants to separate from itself or along its
small fissures, like rifted marriages
or the unpredictable terrain of conversation,
collecting reports in disappearing ink and taking
from previous studies a new story
with which to rail against the current or
conveying information not provided
previously. The information borrowing
brief movements made of rain, these
storms on the horizon now disappear,
and this story of rock resisting and rock succumbing,

the sculpting of ideas and information,
it "reminds us how the earth is shaped,
which rock resists, which succumbs."
This becomes ephemera of the days following,
flowing briefly after the rainfall, appearing
and disappearing, these theories under
punishing sky, under this aged stillness.

One will find this type of evidence briefly during
and after spring rains, the colors dampening,
the light-fall choking, a special quiet awakens,
one feels alone, laughter ceases, the white noise
of the river blends into the sky's quiet, and then
out of this nothing a ripening and then a flowering
of ideas, a plentitude of theories and truths:
obstructions are cleared, pathways founded
and designed as analog to river but sketched in the air,
these meanings of time, space, desire,
brilliance, an unveiling of a drama
with many actors, many plots, these politics, this
dam or this idea of a dam, these sketches
and blue pencil markings, these bulldozers,
scrapers and dump-trucks, these scars on the hillside,
and the smell of disruption, their love
of damaged earth, sweet and delicious,
victims and survivors, entrepreneurs of
the canyon, unseen characters on the periphery
while children smear the chalk-lines, and the rest of us
talk, our arguments like vines in a thicket of blackberry.

35.

The processes of the field—
poppies, delphinium, vetch, little mirrors, little mouths—
can now be called the mysteries of the river. The fan-shaped petals
    reach out in their golden directions.
The canyon's color and the flower's color each proclaim an island of
    their own and a constellated island together.
Also the extract of the flower is a narcotic, a painkiller.
"My household is not modern; it thrives, as the imagination thrives,
    on images."
But these modern flowers love their appliances and transports
and the American's building to its debouchment
like a mighty engineer beside lonely star thistle.
The river opens its bipartisan mouth to all the discarded images.

36.

A story returns, roaring more, then less,
money is the spring that moves the man

for and against
his leveed intentions

the effluent of love and persuasion

cascading and flattening, "my prose
all a bog,"

where there are only a few rivulets

of clear water, mineral dispersing,
injured appendages

under water

BOTANY
tough trunk ceonothus: linear and loved by deer
and serpentine, soap made from flowers

LIBERATION
money from one project diverted to another
we must pause and consider: what is this anger?

The latest revival occurred at a recent show-and-tell for the new spillway under construction at Folsom Dam. Congressman Tom McClintock, R-Auburn, seized the occasion – not so much for congratulations – but to decry recent releases of water from dams on the American River.

"It infuriates me that for the past three days, we have seen releases of water out of dams on the American River triple in order to meet environmental regulations that place the interests of fish above those of human beings."

The congressmen then pivoted and called for the completion of the Auburn Dam, a long stagnant project on the North Fork of the American River originally green-lighted by Congress in 1965, near the end of what the late writer Marc Reisner called the "go-go years" of American dam building. McClintock's colleague from across the aisle, Sacramento Democrat Doris Matsui, sat nearby, shaking her head.

from *Auburn Dam: The Water Project That Won't Die*
Craig Miller, KQED Science
April 30, 2014

37.

The roar above this valley is not the angel of geology it is the angel of forgetting, eroding granite with its tributary paths among berries and fir. This creek beside me issues forth and completes correspondences. The columbine has five sepals forming a tube with a small yellow dot on the opening, an invitation. This letter leaves a trace as the water knows to do.

She will continue to feel that wound until death do us part. Tomorrow will speak with its big mouth. Delphinium decorum is the largest larkspur, five sepals forming a deep purple mouth and four small petals, two white and two blue. The batholith speaks by lifting up and wearing down very slowly. I will continue to feel the wound until death do us part. I expected my father to live longer, maybe forever. A sturdy rain opens and closes on the valley. The mountains are described as "youthful" and "active."

Passing through the kitchen she mentioned that a mild anguish had returned. For a moment I felt the separation of this voice from the waterslide of feeling. I feel responsible for communicating this important information. Paintbrush is deep red and has a two lipped flower growing in bunches from a woody base. It is beloved of the checkerspot butterfly and used as hairwash or a substitute for garlic. The child asked me if there were men in the clouds who made earthquakes. Earthquake-making men, he said.

This mystery begins and ends in rock. The silver lupine's flowers are whorled in clusters. One petal turns from white to yellow to purple as the nectar is drained. In the bedtime story, the two children missed their train and ended up lost in a cave. Lost in a cave without supervision. The next night, I invented a new story. My family is camping and my father and I are searching for a place to pitch a tent. Suddenly we are alone in the wilderness, no one in sight. And suddenly again a bear emerges calmly from behind a boulder, takes my father by the hand, and leads him deeper into the forest. Later, an owl screeched and settled on the branch of a ponderosa.

Growing in bunches from a woody base, right foundation, sturdy construction. The real is easier in the present. Right now a Stellar's Jay is fumbling in the branch of the Jeffrey Pine. Passing through the kitchen she said her mind felt like Ornette Coleman. She may have said "this" pointing to the stereo, "sounds like my mind." The rock outcropping reminds me of multiple snares. Breathing is something I have needed to relearn. Her hands and my hands touching each other. First there is an aspen leaf eddying in a pool beside me and then there isn't.

The angel is filing her tools and whistling. The howling wind in the canyon is a fragment of a larger howl. I walked with that bear in the grove of trees but came back with IVs and baling wire. Meanwhile, the corporation is painting orange lines for new construction in the parking lot. The trees and rocks are nonplussed but tranquil. The mountain quivers to music piped out in loudspeakers. The wind and rain and river and music are in loud correspondence. I am learning to use this listening device. It is a medium I can work with. It puts this flourishing into English. Sometimes poems and calculators can do this work, and sometimes they make gibberish.

38.

"With a mind both weedy and humid"

The disorder embedded
in our married mind—

Not the furnace fire from a hotel hearth,
but dusty blackberry
set to flame, swirling smoke

more than heat.
What was there in her married eyes?

Weedy mind, humid mind:

stop thinking about symbol
When you say *rosaceae,*

Or "sticky potentilla."

To "burst" open, really?

Or, grey pines
beside rapids and serpentine:

wolfish pea
softening the hillside, standing-

still mind for an instant

burst, listen to summer,
sticky mind.

39.

Circle-proud, familied, the ponderosas a covering of changes. Or,
the changes are like colors washing

into one another: birds, window-glass, draperies, beds, pillows,
wallpaper, light fixtures, crying.

All evening the canyon blankets darkness in successive waves, and
the animals return to their special

places. Reflection is common around rivers and lakes. And water
presses down the surface of ravines:

drainage, tears. This system calls to mind every other system: one
new thing enters, gets used,

and finds a way to leave, preferably with some discretion or at least
usefulness to others. Reflection

calms and unnerves. Six branches from two trees elbow and lean
from twig-tip to twig-tip: this feels

like protection: (darkness has sunk there, to the west): where the
changes are, where the river drops,

a trickle and then a pool and then a fall. White flags of yarrow on
the banks: Achilles treated wounds

with it: and others placed it under their pillows to receive visions.
Try to imagine this moment

without reflection or dressings for our wounds. How could some-
one love this canyon enough

to save it without loving his reflection in it: grey pine, manzanita,
wild iris, rock, river, trail.

You pass the river and in a vision you are in commerce with it and its attendant populations, gathering

their needs and histories, and you are bountiful and patient. "We seek to create an environment

in which our creative spirit fits." You imagine these populations as social, playful, violent, competitive,

and full of breathing, sitting, standing still, dissolving, composting: you pass the river thinking aimlessly

of trains, thinking of stations. The place beside the river in which your creative spirit fits. Here, a vision

from Artemis: things in the wild stay wild, worthy and hunted, pregnant; and here a vision from Pan:

things are wild and possessed at once, honored for their earthly music and fitted to humanly love.

40.

Something missing,
perhaps energy,
perhaps the purifying
of time into
entanglement.
The dream pattern
found in geology
and transformed.
Art's false
grandeur: filling

pans with words.
Leaning riverward
into the echoes of
experience being
mined, silty
mind, scraping
voices from
canyon walls.
Sediment, system,
cradling gold.

The river ebbs
and current flows
backward. Bedload
fine, cloudy water.
Red dirt and lumber,
pine construction
under the stars.
Men mostly, away
from home, away
from houses.

Manzanita:
silvery in
moonlight, smooth,

dry slopes, little
apple, made into cider,
mountain driftwood.
River finds itself
in gravity and other
affiliations. Table
its grainy signature

on the bar. The songs
remember her
branches, mind
entrained. Salt
the future. Suffer
the greedy. Worship the flood-
plain.

"Our damming operation has been an entire failure. We
spent many days in constructing the dam, which, when
completed, drained a large portion of the river. When
this was done, we thoroughly prospected the whole, and
found nothing. The banks and bars of the river were
rich in some places, but there was not a grain of gold in
the channel." (Daniel B. Woods, September 7, 1849.
From *Sixteen Months at the Gold Diggings*)

Birthday

June 6

I hear the shimmery voice of morning, lacking comfort, lacking
aspiration. Then the jay hops to the feeder, discovers

emptiness. This mess of episodes and rotting fruit, this story, this
journey of bodies

to outer reaches. Oil on the shores of the Gulf Islands, tar balls in
Pensacola.

This episode is besmeared with poppies, thyme, and mourning
glory, widening

to the oaks and Monterey pines, and our words and syntax,
sentences on top of events as we remember

them, these houses, and the clothing we wore, sunhats and lotions.
Who will share the bodies

Of these things
Who will say good-
Morning and goodnight.
June fog, Deepwater

June 7

The scene outside is silent and muted. The potted plants grow
through the night. The netting is up

for the climbing vines, and the manufactured world is resting. "He
had a pleasing anticipation

of what would be," his marriage to the beautiful flower. Anticipate
health while sunlight banks

the tree-line. The president stands on the shore of Grand Isle, look-
ing out

into the Gulf. My daughter's plastic baby stares at me with her hard
eyes and droopy lashes.

The fabric of the morning rubs and chafes, the usual June fog, light
as a veil, promising

To reveal.
Union
Threading bobbin
Horizon

June 8

What's doubtful, or distant, in this approachable region? If I could
bring my mind to happiness I could seed sorrow

in these clouds. Oil on the banks of Florida. Seems we are adrift.
Aching economy, are you adrift?

The deck birds are searching for the god of fuel, seed-eyed. Wild
strawberry coursing through

the sod. Sparrow with a lung of oil. Little gold seeds in the feeder.
My sleeping girl, kinks in her hair.

She can easily bring her mind into that doubtful, or distant, or
unapproachable region. Effort is your twin,

Your shadowy
Bothersome twin
Mind in array
Harbinger

June 10

Deepest interest, motives of bamboo. They do not suffer, they drink
from the surface, breathe,

and release. BP releases images of the leak and the "underwater
plume." Gushing oil in fitful commerce

with saltwater. In the novel, Fanny rejects the proposal because "it
cannot be *serious*," that word applied

to marriage. She was a serious woman, she was friendly on
Tuesdays, she was a sprouting sunflower,

a menu, a bookmark. The bamboo sits on the porch in containers, a
large slug weighting one slim branch.

Letters arranged, letters embroidered with twofold motives,
un-spelling the objects, un-stitching

The wishes.
Sentenced
In marriages
To pillars

June 13

We raft ourselves to self-made meaning or drown in meaning or
drown in love, framed in photographs,

framed in stories. 1.5 million gallons of oil per day, un-captured
and under water. He will ask his first question

with his eyes. This day in June has just begun, blackberries
blooming along the path, fragile blossoms,

dangerous vines, robins flitting and squawking at the edge of the
frame. Leigh is sleeping and Halina is

Sleeping.
(Bed of clover)
Summer breath
Reckoned earth

June 16

A reverie of sweet remembering, short fits of abstraction—the
president says stopping the spill "has tested the limits

of human technology." We look beyond when we look forward:
this birth we're waiting for, how we will arrive

at this place, not far from where we are now, this orange couch,
clock ticking, airplane above,

clothes folded, garden weeded, appearance of the living boy taking
shape, as I take uneasiness and anger

as a shape within me. We are more than flesh, blood, water, lungs,
and arms. Even his mother, sleeping

here now, cannot know his face, the placement of the cheekbones,
the color of his lips.

Or how he will shoulder a backpack or throw a rock into a river,
how

he will walk the edge of a field or tramp down the middle, how he
will leave, later and finally, how he will

Bring and receive
Gifts.
Incarnadine soul
Ambassador

June 21

Cross-legged in the quiet hours but opening to the day's inventions:
the sunshine was solid

and the sunshine pretended. There goes the winged chariot and its
attendants,

devouring and forgetting names, unspelling words and leaving
letters as compost.

The BP executive is on CSPAN addressing the House Energy
Subcommittee on Oversight and Investigations.

So close to my forty-first birthday, physical life is the chosen life:
that is, a lot of picking up

and putting down, walking the floor with burdens, washing and
repairing. These habits arrive

as a complete and total life, a cloudy dailiness promising sleep.
Schools and bakeries, cafes and flower shops:

settings for stories in which I find purpose or protection from the
revelations I've so artfully

constructed. Today is the summer solstice. I'm thinking of Lake
Clementine, its steep hillsides of dusty

oaks and grey pines, the glassy surface in the morning hours, the
tribute to the WPA project that built the dam.

I flip-flopped past the shimmering marker, star thistle standing
brightly beside my father's deep, dark tan

and glinting sunglasses. If I could change something I would
change my relationship to gratitude.

I would exalt the deserving. Some days clouds would form
mid-morning, some days ripples would form,

Suspended
Traction, blurry
Reversal.
Works, project

June 23

That summer the lake stood still against the water-color oaks. Each morning was orange turning to red

dust caught in the veneer, and we hoped for a breeze among the cut-outs, and yes, we walked in shadows

made by adults, faceless and wretched, practicing distraction in the California evenings: back decks

and barbecues, this real thing made of Manzanita and squirrels but also this copy, this replica of bliss

and siblings, temporary wives, husbands, eyes closed on the back steps beneath constellations,

this experimentation, this art, these happenings off stage, these happenings between persons

after the dishes are dried, intensities in the eyes; or hide-and-seek, standing in the blue light, vulnerable

to discovery; or to be alone, searching for an individual mind while not forgetting the others. Regarding

the objects of memory: constructed things both public and private, shared or unshared, "refreshingly

clear and unforgettably moving," as told to a call-screener or line producer, then drowned in

Dusty
Water.
Withholding
Hereafters

June 24

The light of those days was slow to come, cresting into the deep canyon, not visible but then seemingly on top

of us, noon sky. This was the life that was happening, my father was alive

and driving the boat. Those clouds, those ripples, processes and systems, the smell of

internal combustion mixed with freshwater and fish. Those days predicted these days, for sure,

but they were different, too: my father was not present at my birth, for instance, as I will be present

at the birth of my son, maybe tomorrow, maybe the next day. Still, it was all truth

and his feelings were feelings. His love of the lake was patently obvious, his worries quite distant.

And how I was there in the hospital in Sacramento, my plain red skin on his plain red skin

as the last exhale convulsed his body, abrupt and pleasant, there in the quiet room, there in the floodplain.

Where has he gone to, that symbol and source? He has disappeared into the light,

this center, this father sun and his splintering rays, sometimes in pieces and sometimes

Gone entirely.
Rope-swing
Unknowable
Mercury

June 25

From the scowling jets in the late afternoon, I gorge and settle, private from the body and using that body

Out of breeze and bird-call, distant music, into the flowering of the past and the putting back together.

Swimming is now forbidden along shores of Florida and Mississippi.

I don't know what my father's dreams were. He did not have a priest of even alcohol or music.

He had my mother and his love for others, his garden, his woodshop. We spread his ashes

on the spring equinox beneath a large madrone in Grass Valley. It was shady and a little dark

that morning, and the ashes shined papery white on the layers of peeled bark. He taught me how to run

a lathe and hold a hammer, swing a pick, how to hitch the leg and let the tool's weight do the work—

I've been reading *Mansfield Park* for weeks and finally I've finished. I love the utter bravado

of the last chapter, the way Jane Austen simply admits that she must find simple positive ends for her dreary

characters. And, "Sir Thomas, a parent, and conscious of errors in his own conduct as a parent, was

the longest to suffer." And about Fanny: "She must have been a happy creature in spite of all she felt

Or thought
She felt."
Fearless
Cultivator

June 26

Life as we know it will cease and life as we know it will begin again, probably harder, probably better.

These quiet moments in the early morning, Halina sleeping, Leigh sleeping, the boy still locked inside

of her. There is the need to look away in the face of this bounty, not confident,

not ever, and confused by choices, acceptance of all seems tiring, too much, not virtuous, greedy, wasteful.

Hurricane Alex has severed ties with relief rigs and the oil is spilling unchecked again.

Those roads north of Auburn, their mild climbs, horses and farmhouses, fresh construction, red dirt

and meandering directions leading to dead ends. In those days we would drive out in the convertible just to drive

and talk, park and smoke cigarettes. And we drove to parties. I remember the houses, the rotting shag,

split beam ceilings and untrimmed drywall, plastic toys lying around on linoleum, red dirt and potato bugs.

Terrestrial
Cassette case
The cool flesh
Of an apple

June 28

We make a religion out of accumulating experience and objects, a hymnal of nostalgia and injured toys.

But what I am approaching here is a resolution, the death of a father and the birth of a son, father's day

and birthday, cancer in the dead of winter and regeneration in the heart of summer, the broken ring

and its reparation, simply being who we are in time. You can't step in the same river twice, decay

and rot reconciled by fresh lumber. So the question of happiness raises its irrelevant head, against the maze

of obstacles and shameful practices, and children are simply creatures out of our control passing

through our lives in time, and understood as such, my soon-to-be-born son and my dead father are

journeying outside the lines of my corporeal life though still so clearly here. They are "on my mind." Human

eyes trained to one another, human eyes trained to look away. Lips to be pressed and un-pressed, mouth

emerging. And so, the meal begins, *desayuno*, and this birth that has not happened and will happen, happens again,

And again.
Elemental sunshine
Tiger at the gate
Shaker of houses

Headwater

Mountain lake covers
slimy source-bones.

Today on the trail
you felt your origin

decomposing.
Cottonwood fluff

floated by
with its gauzy bundle

of homeless seeds.
The echo of it

sounded like many
rivers, many skies.

The headwater creates
desire and watches from

above. From there,
among the aspens

and fields of aster, the soul
meanders: there, the source

you cannot have
only to yourself,

and who cannot follow you,
blind river, blind god.

*

Walking up to the headwater of the American from Squaw
Valley, up Shirley Canyon, looking down on hotels and the tram,
restaurants, crunching over bouldering granite along Squaw Creek,
thistle, shooting star, stopping in a shady grove of down trees, wild
grape, bracken, Douglass fir.

Further up, sitting on a granite slab looking down on ski runs, cedars, ponderosas, up to High Camp and Granite Chief in the distance.

Thin cloud-cover, possible storm. Quiet, meaning no cars or people.

Creek crossing, serpentine boulders, aster, delphinium, mosquito buzz. Scrambling over big escarpments, cairns, cooling breeze, tiny Manzanita and white bark pine.

Soft path through old growth firs in a high country meadow, about 7500 feet. A California sister floats by, rocks lying in assembly.

Then climbing switchbacks to the Pacific Crest, 8000 feet, looking forward to the west, the wide opening of the drainage between Granite Chief and Tinker Nob, warm wind blowing through, a few birds.

From the PCT, dropping down northward on the trail about a mile to where the tiny trickle of stream, the north fork of the north fork of the American, crosses the trail.

Setting up camp: tent, stove, hanging the food-bag on an old fir snag. And just then, the thunderstorm rolls in. Everything into the tent! Sitting and reading, drinking mint tea listening to the pitter-patter getting louder and louder until a real storm is happening, heavy rain, pounding thunder, electricity in the air.

*

Source of water!
Voice of water, falling here

Formation of the watershed
Land cut by glaciers

Ravines eroding

At their own large pace,

full-throated thunder.
An ode to massive things:

Wide dark sky
Over Sierra Nevada,

The ache of loneliness,
The incomplete.

*

The sky clears, and birdsong returns.

Call of the red-tail, claiming territory.

(Pay more attention, say the wind spirits.)

A lone Jeffrey Pine right next to the creek before a long straight fall
into the canyon below.

A smallish storm-cloud pregnant with unreleased water.

Pearly everlasting growing outside the tent, stooped with the
burden of rain.

*

Read the contour
of this opening.

Woodpecker ratting
a dead pine.

Many streams, snow-
melt, rain, Sierra

Buttes standing alone.
Then sunset,

darkness, dreaming
in the tent: fires

in all the houses,
burning

from lightening
strike. Is there escape

from these fears
in the night?

You can't fall off
the mountain.

Water can't fall
off the mountain.

To shake the bed-
rock of relevance.

Emptiness engenders
compassion. At 3:00 a.m.

wake to
the sound of

tent flaps, then nothing—
no birds, no

water, no
bears, nothing,

the void and
emergent

moonshine.
From here:

graph of
desire,

birth of
compassion,

origin
in person,

beginning
unending.

Notes

"System and Population" depicts the landscape and history of the American River, and specifically, the proposed damming of the river near Auburn, California. The Auburn Dam project was initially authorized in the 1950's and debate about its construction still continues.

The poems in the sequence sample liberally from many sources, but the primary source of quoted materials comes from Robert Duncan's letters, collected in *The Letters of Robert Duncan and Denise Levertov* (UC Press, 2004).

The quotation from Heraclitus is Daniel Graham's translation.

I would like to thank the Mesa Foundation and the Squaw Valley Community of Writers for their support. Thank you to my dear colleagues, Brenda Hillman and Matthew Zapruder. Thanks to Leigh and Halina and Luke for endless inspiration. For my parents and brothers and sisters, who took me to the river.

Free Verse Editions

Edited by Jon Thompson

13 ways of happily by Emily Carr
Between the Twilight and the Sky by Jennie Neighbors
Blood Orbits by Ger Killeen
The Bodies by Chris Sindt
The Book of Isaac by Aidan Semmens
Canticle of the Night Path by Jennifer Atkinson
Child in the Road by Cindy Savett
Condominium of the Flesh by Valerio Magrelli, trans. by Clarissa Botsford
Contrapuntal by Christopher Kondrich
Country Album by James Capozzi
The Curiosities by Brittany Perham
Current by Lisa Fishman
Dismantling the Angel by Eric Pankey
Divination Machine by F. Daniel Rzicznek
Erros by Morgan Lucas Schuldt
Fifteen Seconds without Sorrow by Shim Bo-Seon, translated by Chung Eun-Gwi and Brother Anthony of Taizé
The Forever Notes by Ethel Rackin
The Flying House by Dawn-Michelle Baude
Go On by Ethel Rackin
Instances: Selected Poems by Jeongrye Choi, translated by Brenda Hillman, Wayne de Fremery, & Jeongrye Choi
The Magnetic Brackets by Jesús Losada, translated by Michael Smith & Luis Ingelmo
Man Praying by Donald Platt
A Map of Faring by Peter Riley
No Shape Bends the River So Long by Monica Berlin & Beth Marzoni
Overyellow, by Nicolas Pesquès, translated by Cole Swensen
Physis by Nicolas Pesque, translated by Cole Swensen
Pilgrimage Suites by Derek Gromadzki
Pilgrimly by Siobhán Scarry
Poems from above the Hill & Selected Work by Ashur Etwebi, translated by Brenda Hillman & Diallah Haidar
The Prison Poems by Miguel Hernández, translated by Michael Smith
Puppet Wardrobe by Daniel Tiffany
Quarry by Carolyn Guinzio

About the Author

Christopher Sindt is the author of *The Bodies*, published by Parlor Press's Free Verse Editions, and a chapbook of poetry, *The Land of Give and Take*. His work has appeared recently in *Free Verse, nocturnes, Pool, Swerve, Xantippe* and other publications. He received the James D. Phelan Award from the San Francisco Foundation and residencies at the MacDowell Colony, Mesa Refuge, and the Blue Mountain Center. He teaches at Saint Mary's College of California.

Photograph of the author.

www.ingramcontent.com/pod-product-compliance
Lightning Source LLC
Chambersburg PA
CBHW022033090426
42741CB00007B/1044